Table of Contents

This lesson plan book belongs to:

Name _____

School _____

Grade/Subject _____

Room _____

School Year _____

Address _____

Phone _____

Teacher Created Resources, Inc.
6421 Industry Way
Westminster, CA 92683
www.teachercreated.com

ISBN: **978-1-4206-4549-1**

©2007 Teacher Created Resources, Inc.
Reprinted, 2015

Made in U.S.A.

Managing Editor/Creative Director:
Karen Goldfluss, M.S. Ed.

Art Production Manager: Kevin Barnes

Cover Design: Denise Bauer

Imaging: James Edward Grace
Len Swierski

Publisher: Mary D. Smith, M.S. Ed.

©Debbie Mumm
www.debbiemumm.com

Ways to Use This Book

Seating Chart (page 3)

A seating chart is provided for easy reference. Table and desk arrangements will vary throughout the year depending on room size, available furniture, grade level taught, teaching style, and academic program needs.

To accommodate a variety of classroom arrangements, you may wish to create additional charts and place specific seating information in a separate folder.

Student Roster (pages 4 – 7)

Use the roster to record information for each student. Having the roster in your lesson plan book provides you with quick and easy access to important data for both you and a substitute teacher.

Our Weekly Schedule (page 8)

If your schedule changes periodically, you may wish to duplicate this page before completing your current schedule. Attach new schedules throughout the year, as the need arises.

Year At A Glance (page 9)

Use this chart to plan units of study and/or to focus on immediate and upcoming events, conferences, meetings, seminars, and other important dates. Record each event as soon as you are notified.

The Year At A Glance chart can also be reproduced for students to help them plan projects and keep track of important dates and events.

Substitute Teacher Information (pages 10 and 11)

Document all pertinent information on these pages. If you have a copy of the layout of your school, attach it to page 11. Otherwise, sketch a diagram of the school building and grounds.

Be sure to show important locations, such as the office, restrooms, faculty lounge, cafeteria, auditorium, and playground.

Including the Standards (pages 12 – 15)

Most teachers are required to write lesson plans each week, but in many school districts, lesson plans alone are no longer considered enough. A majority of school systems now require teachers to include the standards addressed in each lesson along with their regular lesson plans.

Staying on Track

A lesson book provides the teacher with a convenient and compact outline of the week's plans. The growing trend among most educators is to document the use of standards by including them with lessons. However, lesson plan books generally cannot provide adequate space for teachers to record both lesson plans and standards. An easy-to-use standards form that complements a teacher's lesson plans is a handy tool for "staying on track."

Pages 12 through 15 provide the teacher with general information about the standards, a listing of several national standards organizations, and a handy form for recording standards that correlate with weekly plans.

About the Standards Form

A sample form for recording weekly standards is provided on page 14. The blank form on page 15 can be reproduced and used to record standards for any grade level or subject. This page can also be conveniently attached to any lesson plans that are required to be submitted to an administrator. Another great way to use the standards form is to make multiple copies and keep them in a binder along with related material on standards.

Lesson Plans (pages 16 – 95)

Use this section to help you organize your lesson plans each week. There are enough weekly plan pages to cover a 40-week school year. At the top of the left-hand page, fill in the blank to indicate the week dates for which the plans are written. The first column may be used for notes.

For special programs requiring more in-depth explanation of plans, reference the specific folder, notebook, guide, etc., to which the teacher should be directed. This is especially helpful to substitute teachers.

Seating Chart

Seat Arrangement Ideas

The size and shape of your room will play a large part in your seating arrangement.

You may want to change this layout once you are familiar with your students and their needs.

Regardless of your seating plan, the most important concern is that you can easily see all your students and the children in turn have good visibility of you, the board, and other focal points in the room.

1. Basic Row Seating

2. U-Shaped Seating

3. Rectangular Seating

4. V-Shaped Seating

5. Cluster Seating
(Desks or Tables)

6. Partner Seating

	Names	Phone	Address
1	Student .... Parent	H W Other	
2	Student .... Parent	H W Other	
3	Student .... Parent	H W Other	
4	Student .... Parent	H W Other	
5	Student .... Parent	H W Other	
6	Student .... Parent	H W Other	
7	Student .... Parent	H W Other	
8	Student .... Parent	H W Other	
9	Student .... Parent	H W Other	
10	Student .... Parent	H W Other	
11	Student .... Parent	H W Other	
12	Student .... Parent	H W Other	
13	Student .... Parent	H W Other	
14	Student .... Parent	H W Other	
15	Student .... Parent	H W Other	
16	Student .... Parent	H W Other	

Roster

Birthday	Siblings	Notes

 #4549 Lesson Plan Book

	Names	Phone	Address
17	Student Parent	H W Other	
18	Student Parent	H W Other	
19	Student Parent	H W Other	
20	Student Parent	H W Other	
21	Student Parent	H W Other	
22	Student Parent	H W Other	
23	Student Parent	H W Other	
24	Student Parent	H W Other	
25	Student Parent	H W Other	
26	Student Parent	H W Other	
27	Student Parent	H W Other	
28	Student Parent	H W Other	
29	Student Parent	H W Other	
30	Student Parent	H W Other	
31	Student Parent	H W Other	
32	Student Parent	H W Other	

Roster

Birthday	Siblings	Notes

Our Weekly Schedule

Time	Monday	Tuesday	Wednesday	Thursday	Friday

Year at a Glance

AUGUST	SEPTEMBER	OCTOBER
NOVEMBER	DECEMBER	JANUARY
FEBRUARY	MARCH	APRIL
MAY	JUNE	JULY

Substitute Teacher

School Schedule

- Class Begins _____
- Morning Recess _____
- Lunchtime _____
- Class Resumes _____
- Afternoon Recess _____
- Dismissal _____

Special Notes

_____
_____
_____
_____
_____
_____
_____
_____

Special Classes

Student _____
Class _____ Day _____ Time_____
Student _____
Class _____ Day _____ Time_____
Student _____
Class _____ Day _____Time_____

Where to Find

- Class List _____
- School Layout _____
- Seating Chart _____
- Attendance Record _____
- Lesson Plans_____
- Teacher Manuals_____
- First Aid Kit _____
- Emergency Information_____
- Supplementary Activities_____
- Class Supplies–paper, pencils, etc. _____
- Referral forms and procedures_____

_____
_____
_____
_____
_____
_____
_____
_____
_____

Special Needs Students

Student	Needs	Time and Place
_____	_____	_____
_____	_____	_____
_____	_____	_____
_____	_____	_____
_____	_____	_____
_____	_____	_____
_____	_____	_____

Information

Classroom Standards

- When finished with an assignment

  _____

  _____

- When and how to speak out in class

  _____

  _____

- Incentive Program

  _____

  _____

- Discipline

  _____

  _____

- Restroom Procedure

  _____

  _____

People Who Can Help

- Teacher/Room _____

- Dependable Students _____

  _____

  _____

  _____

  _____

  _____

- Principal _____

- Secretary _____

- Custodian _____

- Counselor _____

- Nurse _____

Map of Our School

Including the Standards

❏ *Stop and Go: Standards and Benchmarks*

Educational standards provide teachers with written expectations of what they need to teach during a school year. Standards are most often conveniently divided by grade level and subject matter. For example, a teacher in a fifth grade social studies class might be given a standard that states he or she is responsible for teaching students important historical figures from the Civil War era such as Abraham Lincoln, Frederick Douglas, and Robert E. Lee. The teacher uses the standard to know what to teach, but she then applies a benchmark to assess whether the students learned the standard. A benchmark might be anything from an oral report to a short quiz. Whatever the teacher decides to use to assess the learning, this benchmark helps her decide whether to stop and teach the standard again or whether to go on to the next standard listed in the guidelines.

❏ *Who's Giving Directions?*

So where do all these directions or guidelines come from, and how do you know which ones to use?

Back in the 1980's there was a move across the United States to standardize education in the core subject areas. It was a movement to ensure that students were headed in the same direction no matter who was giving the directions.

Individual states created frameworks or standards for different subjects and grade levels. Some of the standards overlapped from one grade level to the next. Some were divided into levels such as standards that were just being introduced at a grade level, standards that were developing at a grade level, and standards that should be mastered at a grade level. But there was a push for something more; national standards for all states to look at were also being created. These national standards provided a way for state educational departments to be sure their students were meeting the same goals as students throughout the United States— in effect, creating a "standardization of standards" on a national level.

❏ *Filling Up on Information*

With today's easy Internet access, a vast amount of information is available to those educators willing to take the time to look and learn. National standards for core subject areas can be accessed by researching some of the following organizations and visiting their websites.

> **Common Core State Standards Initiative (CCSS)**
> http://www.corestandards.org/
>
> **National Council of Teachers of Mathematics (NCTM)**
> http://www.nctm.org/
>
> **National Council of Teachers of English (NCTE)**
> http://www.ncte.org/
>
> **National Council for the Social Studies (NCSS)**
> http://www.ncss.org/
>
> **National Science Teachers Association (NSTA)**
> http://www.nsta.org/standards
>
> **National Council for Geographic Education (NCGE)**
> http://www.ncge.org/standards
>
> **Mid-Continent Research for Education and Learning (McREL)**
> http://www.mcrel.org/

Including the Standards *(cont.)*

❏ *Filling Up on Information (cont.)*

For a comprehensive and easy-to-use reference of additional national standards as well as a link to state standards, go to the Education world® website (http://www.educationworld.com/standards/). There you will find standards for Fine Arts, Language Arts, Math, Physical Education and Health, Science, Social Studies, and Technology.

Yet another resource to fill up on information is McREL or Mid-continent Research for Education and Learning. Known as a "Compendium of Standards and Benchmarks", this resource is well-researched. It includes standards and benchmarks that represent a consolidation of national and state standards in several content areas for grades K through 12. (The McREL website is http://www.mcrel.org/.)

❏ *Standards: Shifting into Drive*

The first time you sat behind the wheel of a car, it was exhilarating. You were the driver. You were in control. You were ready to take off down the highway of life. But then, something happened. Where was first gear? How did you end up in third gear? Was that the clutch your foot was on or had you hit the break? Then you and your dream machine "jumped" about three feet before shutting off the engine. It was then that you understood–maybe this wasn't going to be so easy after all. If only you could have turned that standard car in for an automatic, how much easier it would have been to learn how to drive!

In education, identifying and applying standards can be just as frustrating at times as those standard cars driven by first-time drivers. And yet, once you caught on, you realized the car had a logical pattern: first gear, second gear, third gear, and so on. Educational standards also make sense, and just like that standard vehicle, those educational standards can take you and your students in the direction you want and need to go once you learn how to apply them.

❏ *Ready, Set, Go!*

What are standards, and why do we need them in education? A standard is a criteria or a guideline. Standards in education allow you to make a judgment about what a child should be able to do at a certain grade level, and once you've determined what he or she should be able to do, you can then help the child achieve educational goals.

Without this educational map, many teachers and students might continue on a path headed in the wrong direction. If you were taking a trip to your favorite vacation spot, you wouldn't go without first making a plan. Educators must also have a plan to ensure that their educational goals are heading in the right direction. This is where standards really help put us in the driver's seat and get us ready to go.

Weekly Standards (Sample)

Name: _____

Class/Subject	Day	Date	Standards	Benchmarks	Class Avg.	Reteach
Math	M	3/11	Multiply 2 digit numbers	10 question quiz	65%	(Y) N
	T	3/12	Multiply 2 digit numbers	New quiz	85%	Y (N)
	W	3/13	No new standard	N/A	N/A	Y N
	TH	3/14	(begin) multiply with decimals	Exit cards	69%	(Y) N
	F	3/15	(review both standards)	Art activity w/multiple)	N/A	Y N
Science	M	3/18	Know the order of the planets	Quiz - list header	95%	(Y) N
	T	3/19	No new standard	N/A	N/A	Y N
	W	3/20	Know the order of the planets	Make mobiles	N/A	Y N
	TH	3/21	Assembly (no science)			Y N
	F	3/22	Know the order of the planets	Science movie & quiz	98%	Y (N)
Spelling	M	3/25	Spell words that have prefixes			Y N
	T	3/26	Spell words that have prefixes	Pretest	63%	(Y) N
	W	3/27	Spell words that have prefixes/Use words correctly in context	Homework sheet	82%	(Y) N
	TH	3/28	Spell words that have prefixes	Test	89%	Y (N)
	F	3/29	No class (school-wide assembly)			Y N
	M					Y N
	T					Y N
	W					Y N
	TH					Y N
	F					Y N
	M					Y N
	T					Y N
	W					Y N
	TH					Y N
	F					Y N
	M					Y N
	T					Y N
	W					Y N
	TH					Y N
	F					Y N

Note: This teacher does not teach Reading, Language Arts, or Social Studies, however the chart can accommodate up to six subjects.

Weekly Standards

Name:

Class/Subject	Day	Date	Standards	Benchmarks	Class Avg.	Reteach
	M					Y N
	T					Y N
	W					Y N
	TH					Y N
	F					Y N
	M					Y N
	T					Y N
	W					Y N
	TH					Y N
	F					Y N
	M					Y N
	T					Y N
	W					Y N
	TH					Y N
	F					Y N
	M					Y N
	T					Y N
	W					Y N
	TH					Y N
	F					Y N
	M					Y N
	T					Y N
	W					Y N
	TH					Y N
	F					Y N
	M					Y N
	T					Y N
	W					Y N
	TH					Y N
	F					Y N

Subject/Time			
MONDAY			
TUESDAY			
WEDNESDAY			
THURSDAY			
FRIDAY			

Subject/Time		
MONDAY		
TUESDAY		
WEDNESDAY		
THURSDAY		
FRIDAY		

Subject/Time		
MONDAY		
TUESDAY		
WEDNESDAY		
THURSDAY		
FRIDAY		

Week of _____

Subject/Time		
MONDAY		
TUESDAY		
WEDNESDAY		
THURSDAY		
FRIDAY		

Subject/Time			
MONDAY			
TUESDAY			
WEDNESDAY			
THURSDAY			
FRIDAY			

Week of _____

Subject/Time			
MONDAY			
TUESDAY			
WEDNESDAY			
THURSDAY			
FRIDAY			

26

Subject/Time			
MONDAY			
TUESDAY			
WEDNESDAY			
THURSDAY			
FRIDAY			

28

Subject/Time		
MONDAY		
TUESDAY		
WEDNESDAY		
THURSDAY		
FRIDAY		

Subject/Time			
MONDAY			
TUESDAY			
WEDNESDAY			
THURSDAY			
FRIDAY			

Subject/Time			
MONDAY			
TUESDAY			
WEDNESDAY			
THURSDAY			
FRIDAY			

Subject/Time		
MONDAY		
TUESDAY		
WEDNESDAY		
THURSDAY		
FRIDAY		

Subject/Time			
MONDAY			
TUESDAY			
WEDNESDAY			
THURSDAY			
FRIDAY			

Subject/Time			
MONDAY			
TUESDAY			
WEDNESDAY			
THURSDAY			
FRIDAY			

Subject/Time		
MONDAY		
TUESDAY		
WEDNESDAY		
THURSDAY		
FRIDAY		

Subject/Time

MONDAY

TUESDAY

WEDNESDAY

THURSDAY

FRIDAY

Subject/Time			
MONDAY			
TUESDAY			
WEDNESDAY			
THURSDAY			
FRIDAY			

Subject/Time			
MONDAY			
TUESDAY			
WEDNESDAY			
THURSDAY			
FRIDAY			

Subject/Time			
MONDAY			
TUESDAY			
WEDNESDAY			
THURSDAY			
FRIDAY			

Week of _____

Subject/Time			
MONDAY			
TUESDAY			
WEDNESDAY			
THURSDAY			
FRIDAY			

Subject/Time			
MONDAY			
TUESDAY			
WEDNESDAY			
THURSDAY			
FRIDAY			

Subject/Time			
MONDAY			
TUESDAY			
WEDNESDAY			
THURSDAY			
FRIDAY			

Subject/Time			
MONDAY			
TUESDAY			
WEDNESDAY			
THURSDAY			
FRIDAY			

58

Subject/Time		
MONDAY		
TUESDAY		
WEDNESDAY		
THURSDAY		
FRIDAY		

Subject/Time

MONDAY

TUESDAY

WEDNESDAY

THURSDAY

FRIDAY

Week of _____

Subject/Time			
MONDAY			
TUESDAY			
WEDNESDAY			
THURSDAY			
FRIDAY			

Week of _____

Subject/Time			
MONDAY			
TUESDAY			
WEDNESDAY			
THURSDAY			
FRIDAY			

Subject/Time		
MONDAY		
TUESDAY		
WEDNESDAY		
THURSDAY		
FRIDAY		

Subject/Time

MONDAY

TUESDAY

WEDNESDAY

THURSDAY

FRIDAY

Week of _____

Subject/Time			
MONDAY			
TUESDAY			
WEDNESDAY			
THURSDAY			
FRIDAY			

72

Week of _____

Subject/Time			
MONDAY			
TUESDAY			
WEDNESDAY			
THURSDAY			
FRIDAY			

Subject/Time			
MONDAY			
TUESDAY			
WEDNESDAY			
THURSDAY			
FRIDAY			

Subject/Time			
MONDAY			
TUESDAY			
WEDNESDAY			
THURSDAY			
FRIDAY			

Subject/Time		
MONDAY		
TUESDAY		
WEDNESDAY		
THURSDAY		
FRIDAY		

Week of _____

Subject/Time		
MONDAY		
TUESDAY		
WEDNESDAY		
THURSDAY		
FRIDAY		

Week of _____

Subject/Time		
MONDAY		
TUESDAY		
WEDNESDAY		
THURSDAY		
FRIDAY		

Subject/Time			
MONDAY			
TUESDAY			
WEDNESDAY			
THURSDAY			
FRIDAY			

Subject/Time

MONDAY

TUESDAY

WEDNESDAY

THURSDAY

FRIDAY

Subject/Time		
MONDAY		
TUESDAY		
WEDNESDAY		
THURSDAY		
FRIDAY		

Subject/Time

MONDAY

TUESDAY

WEDNESDAY

THURSDAY

FRIDAY

Subject/Time

MONDAY

TUESDAY

WEDNESDAY

THURSDAY

FRIDAY

Notes

96